Pope Benedictus XV

St. Jerome and Holy Scripture

The Encyclical Letter of Our Holy Father, Pope Benedict XV

Pope Benedictus XV

St. Jerome and Holy Scripture
The Encyclical Letter of Our Holy Father, Pope Benedict XV

ISBN/EAN: 9783337100919

Printed in Europe, USA, Canada, Australia, Japan

Cover: Foto ©Lupo / pixelio.de

More available books at **www.hansebooks.com**

ST. JEROME AND HOLY SCRIPTURE

THE ENCYCLICAL LETTER OF OUR
HOLY FATHER, POPE BENEDICT XV
TO ALL PATRIARCHS, PRIMATES, ARCHBISHOPS,
BISHOPS AND ORDINARIES IN UNION WITH THE
APOSTOLIC SEE: ON THE FIFTEENTH CENTENARY
of the DEATH *of* ST. JEROME, DOCTOR *of* HOLY CHURCH

AUTHORISED TRANSLATION

P. J. KENEDY AND SONS
44, BARCLAY STREET, NEW YORK

CONTENTS

v

D

E

F

G

St. Jerome and Holy Scripture

A

St. Jerome's Life and Labours

SINCE the Holy Spirit, the Comforter, had bestowed
the Scriptures on the human race for their instruction
in Divine things, He also raised up in successive
ages saintly and learned men whose task it should be to
develop that treasure and so provide for the faithful
plenteous "consolation from the Scriptures."[1]   Foremost
among these teachers stands St. Jerome.   Him the
Catholic Church acclaims and reveres as her "Greatest
Doctor," divinely given her for the understanding of the
Bible.   And now that the fifteenth centenary of his death
is approaching we would not willingly let pass so
favourable an opportunity of addressing you on the debt
we owe him.   For the responsibility of our Apostolic
office impels us to set before you his wonderful example
and so promote the study of Holy Scripture in accordance
with the teaching of our predecessors, Leo XIII. and
Pius X., which we desire to apply more precisely still to
the present needs of the Church.   For St. Jerome—
"strenuous Catholic, learned in the Scriptures,"[2] "teacher

---

[1] Rom. xv. 4.   [2] Sulpicius Severus, *Dial.* i. 7.

of Catholics,"[1] "model of virtue, world's teacher"[2]—has by his earnest and illuminative defence of Catholic doctrine on Holy Scripture left us most precious instructions. These we propose to set before you and so promote among the children of the Church, and especially among the clergy, assiduous and reverent study of the Bible.

No need to remind you, Venerable Brethren, that Jerome was born in Stridonia, in a town "on the borders of Dalmatia and Pannonia";[3] that from his infancy he was brought up a Catholic;[4] that after his baptism here in Rome[5] he lived to an advanced age and devoted all his powers to studying, expounding, and defending the Bible. At Rome he had learned Latin and Greek, and hardly had he left the school of rhetoric than he ventured on a Commentary on Abdias the Prophet. This "youthful piece of work"[6] kindled in him such love of the Bible that he decided—like the man in the Gospel who found a treasure—to spurn "any emoluments the world could provide,"[7] and devote himself wholly to such studies. Nothing could deter him from this stern resolve. He left home, parents, sister, and relatives; he denied himself the more delicate food he had been accustomed to, and went to the East so that he might gather from studious reading of the Bible the fuller riches of Christ and true knowledge of his Saviour.[8] Jerome himself tells us in several places how assiduously he toiled :

---

[1] Cassian, *De inc.* vii. 26.
[2] S. Prosper, *Carmen de Ingratis* v. 57.
[3] *Vir. Illustr.* cxxxv.
[4] *Ep.* lxxxii. 2.   [5] *Ep.* xv. 1; xvi. 2.
[6] *Præf. in* Abdiam.   [7] *In* Matt. xiii. 14.
[8] *Ep.* xxii. 30.

"An eager desire to learn obsessed me. But I was not so foolish as to try and teach myself. At Antioch I regularly attended the lectures of Apollinarius of Laodicea ; but while I learned much from him about the Bible, I would never accept his doubtful teachings about its interpretation."[1]

From Antioch he betook himself to the desert of Chalcis, in Syria, to perfect himself in his knowledge of the Bible, and at the same time to curb "youthful desires" by means of hard study. Here he engaged a convert Jew to teach him Hebrew and Chaldaic.

"What a toil it was ! How difficult I found it ! How often I was on the point of giving it up in despair, and yet in my eagerness to learn took it up again ! Myself can bear witness of this, and so, too, can those who had lived with me at the time. Yet I thank God for the fruit I won from that bitter seed."[2]

Lest, however, he should grow idle in this desert where there were no heretics to vex him, Jerome betook himself to Constantinople, where for nearly three years he studied Holy Scripture under St. Gregory the Theologian, then Bishop of that See and in the height of his fame as a teacher. While there he translated into Latin Origen's *Homilies on the Prophets* and Eusebius' *Chronicle ;* he also wrote on Isaias' vision of the Seraphim. He then returned to Rome on ecclesiastical business, and Pope Damasus admitted him into his court.[3] However, he let nothing distract from continual occupation with the Bible,[4] and the task of copying various manuscripts,[5]

---

[1] *Ep.* lxxxiv. 3.   [2] *Ep.* cxxv. 12.
[3] *Ep.* cxxiii. 9 ; cxxvii. 7.   [4] *Ep.* cxxvii. 7.
[5] *Ep.* xxxvi. 1 ; *cf.* xxxii. 1.

as well as answering the many questions put to him by students of both sexes.[1]

Pope Damasus had entrusted to him a most laborious task, the correction of the Latin text of the Bible. So well did Jerome carry this out that even to-day men versed in such studies appreciate its value more and more. But he ever yearned for Palestine, and when the Pope died he retired to Bethlehem to a monastery nigh to the cave where Christ was born. Every moment he could spare from prayer he gave to Biblical studies.

" Though my hair was now growing grey and though I looked more like professor than student, yet I went to Alexandria to attend Didymus' lectures. I owe him much. What I did not know I learned. What I knew already I did not lose through his different presentation of it. Men thought I had done with tutors ; but when I got back to Jerusalem and Bethlehem how hard I worked and what a price I paid for my night-time teacher Baraninus! Like another Nicodemus he was afraid of the Jews !"[2]

Nor was Jerome content merely to gather up this or that teacher's words ; he gathered from all quarters whatever might prove of use to him in his task. From the outset he had accumulated the best possible copies of the Bible and the best commentators on it, but now he worked on copies from the synagogues and from the library formed at Cæsarea by Origen and Eusebius ; he hoped by assiduous comparison of texts to arrive at greater certainty touching the actual text and its meaning. With this same purpose he went all through Palestine.

[1] *Ep.* xlv. 2 ; *cf.* cxxvi. 3 ; cxxvii. 7.
[2] *Ep.* lxxxiv. 3.

For he was thoroughly convinced of the truth of what he once wrote to Domnio and Rogatian :

" A man will understand the Bible better if he has seen Judæa with his own eyes and discovered its ancient cities and sites either under the old names or newer ones. In company with some learned Hebrews I went through the entire land the names of whose sites are on every Christian's lips."[1]

He nourished his soul unceasingly on this most pleasant food : he explained St. Paul's Epistles ; he corrected the Latin version of the Old Testament by the Greek ; he translated afresh nearly all the books of the Old Testament from Hebrew into Latin ; day by day he discussed Biblical questions with the brethren who came to him, and answered letters on Biblical questions which poured in upon him from all sides ; besides all this, he was constantly refuting men who assailed Catholic doctrine and unity. Indeed, such was his love for Holy Scripture that he ceased not from writing or dictating till his hand stiffened in death and his voice was silent for ever. So it was that, sparing himself neither labour nor watching nor expense, he continued to extreme old age meditating day and night beside the Crib on the Law of the Lord ; of greater profit to the Catholic cause by his life and example in his solitude than if he had passed his life at Rome, the capital of the world.

[1] *Præf. in* 1 Paral.

B

His Teaching regarding Holy Scripture

(*a*) ITS PLENARY INSPIRATION

AFTER this preliminary account of St. Jerome's life and labours we may now treat of his teaching on the divine dignity and absolute truth of Scripture. You will not find a page in his writings which does not show clearly that he, in common with the whole Catholic Church, firmly and consistently held that the Sacred Books—written as they were under the inspiration of the Holy Spirit—have God for their Author, and as such were delivered to the Church. Thus he asserts that the Books of the Bible were composed at the inspiration, or suggestion, or even at the dictation of the Holy Spirit; even that they were written and edited by Him. Yet he never questions but that the individual authors of these Books worked in full freedom under the Divine afflatus, each of them in accordance with their individual nature and character. Thus he is not merely content to affirm as a general principle—what indeed pertains to all the sacred writers—that they followed the Spirit of God as they wrote, in such sort that God is the principal cause of all that Scripture means and says; but he also accurately descries what pertains to each individual writer. In each case Jerome shows us how, in composition, in language, in style and mode of expression, each of them uses his own gifts and powers ; hence he is able to portray and describe for us their individual character, almost their very features ; this is especially so in his treatment of the Prophets and of St. Paul. This partnership of God and man in the production of a work in common Jerome illustrates by the case of a workman who uses instruments for the production of his work ; for he says that whatsoever the sacred authors say

"Is the word of God, and not their own ; and what the Lord says by their mouths He says, as it were, by means of an instrument."[1]

If we ask how we are to explain this power and action of God, the principal cause, on the sacred writers we shall find that St. Jerome in no wise differs from the common teaching of the Catholic Church. For he holds that God, through His grace, illumines the writer's mind regarding the particular truth which, "in the person of God," he is to set before men ; he holds, moreover, that God moves the writer's will—nay, even impels it—to write ; finally, that God abides with him unceasingly, in unique fashion, until his task is accomplished. Whence the Saint infers the supreme excellence and dignity of Scripture, and declares that knowledge of it is to be likened to the "treasure "[2] and the "pearl beyond price,"[3] since in them are to be found the riches of Christ[4] and "silver wherewith to adorn God's house."[5]

---

[1] *Tract. in* Ps. lxxxviii.
[2] *Comment. in* Matt. xiii. 4.
[3] *Ibid.* xiii. 45.
[4] *Quæst. in Genesim, Prologus.*
[5] *Comment. in* Aggæum, ii. 1 ; *cf. in* Gal. ii. 10.

(*b*) ITS AUTHORITATIVE CHARACTER

Jerome also insists on the supereminent authority of Scripture. When controversy arose he had recourse to the Bible as a storehouse of arguments, and he used its testimony as a weapon for refuting his adversaries' arguments, because he held that the Bible's witness afforded solid and irrefutable arguments. Thus, when Helvidius denied the perpetual virginity of the Mother of God, Jerome was content simply to reply :

" Just as we do not deny these things which are written, so do we repudiate things that are not written. That God was born of a Virgin we believe, because we read it. That Mary was married after His birth we do not believe because we do not read it."[1]

In the same fashion he undertakes to defend against Jovinian, with precisely the same weapons, the Catholic doctrines of the virginal state, of perseverance, of abstinence, and of the merit of good works :

" In refuting his statements I shall rely especially on the testimony of Scripture, lest he should grumble and complain that he has been vanquished rather by my eloquence than by the truth."[2]

So, too, when defending himself against the same Helvidius, he says : " He was, you might say, begged to yield to me, and be led away as a willing and unresisting captive in the bonds of truth."[3] Again, " We must not follow the errors of our parents, nor of those who have gone before us; we have the authority of the Scriptures

---

[1] *Adv. Helvid.* xix.   [2] *Adv. Jovin.* i. 4.
[3] *Ep.* xlix. (xlviii.) 14, 1.

and God's teaching to command us."[1] Once more, when showing Fabiola how to deal with critics, he says:

" When you are really instructed in the Divine Scriptures, and have realised that its laws and testimonies are the bonds of truth, then you can contend with adversaries ; then you will fetter them and lead them bound into captivity ; then of the foes you have made captive you will make freedmen of God."[2]

(c) ITS IMMUNITY FROM ERROR

Jerome further shews that the immunity of Scripture from error or deception is necessarily bound up with its Divine inspiration and supreme authority. He says he had learnt this in the most celebrated schools, whether of East or West, and that it was taught him as the doctrine of the Fathers, and generally received. Thus when, at the instance of Pope Damasus, he had begun correcting the Latin text of the New Testament, and certain " manikins " had vehemently attacked him for " making corrections in the Gospels in face of the authority of the Fathers and of general opinion," Jerome briefly replied that he was not so utterly stupid nor so grossly uneducated as to imagine that the Lord's words needed any correction or were not divinely inspired.[3] Similarly, when explaining Ezechiel's first vision as portraying the *Four Gospels*, he remarks :

" That the entire body and the back were full of eyes will be plain to anybody who realises that there is nought in the Gospels which does not shine and illumine the

[1] *Comment. in* Jer. ix. 12. [2] *Ep.* lxxviii. 30.
[3] *Ep.* xxvii. 1.

world by its splendour, so that even things that seem trifling and unimportant shine with the majesty of the Holy Spirit."[1]

What he has said here of the Gospels he applies in his Commentaries to the rest of the Lord's words ; he regards it as the very rule and foundation of Catholic interpretation ; indeed, for Jerome, a true prophet was to be distinguished from a false by this very note of truth :[2] " The Lord's words are true ; for Him to say it means that it is."[3]   Again, " Scripture cannot lie ";[4] it is wrong to say Scripture lies,[5] nay, it is impious even to admit the very notion of error where the Bible is concerned.[6]   " The Apostles," he says, " are one thing ; other writers "—that is, profane writers—" are another "; " the former always tell the truth ; the latter—as being mere men—sometimes err,"[7] and though many things are said in the Bible which seem incredible, yet they are true;[8] in this " word of truth " you cannot find things or statements which are contradictory, " there is nothing discordant nor conflicting " ;[9]   consequently, " when Scripture seems to be in conflict with itself both passages are true despite their diversity."[10]

Holding principles like these, Jerome was compelled, when he discovered apparent discrepancies in the Sacred Books, to use every endeavour to unravel the difficulty. If he felt that he had not satisfactorily settled the problem,

---

[1] *In* Ezech. i. 15.
[2] *In* Mich. ii. 11; iii. 5.
[3] *In* Mich. iv. 1.
[4] *In* Jer. xxxi. 35.
[5] *In* Nah. i. 9.
[6] *Ep.* lvii. 7.
[7] *Ep.* lxxxii. 7.
[8] *Ep.* lxxii. 2.
[9] *Ep.* xviii. 7; *cf.* xlvi. 6.
[10] *Ep.* xxxvi. 11.

he would return to it again and again, not always, indeed, with the happiest results. Yet he would never accuse the sacred writers of the slightest mistake—" that we leave to impious folk like Celsus, Porphyry, and Julian."[1] Here he is in full agreement with Augustine, who wrote to Jerome that to the Sacred Books alone had he been wont to accord such honour and reverence as firmly to believe that none of their writers had ever fallen into any error ; and that consequently, if in the said books he came across anything which seemed to run counter to the truth, he did not think that that was really the case, but either that his copy was defective or that the translator had made a mistake, or again, that he himself had failed to understand. He continues :

" Nor do I deem that you think otherwise. Indeed, I absolutely decline to think that you would have people read your own books in the same way as they read those of the Prophets and Apostles ; the idea that these latter could contain any errors is impious."[2]

St. Jerome's teaching on this point serves to confirm and illustrate what our predecessor of happy memory, Leo XIII., declared to be the ancient and traditional belief of the Church touching the absolute immunity of Scripture from error :

" So far is it from being the case that error can be compatible with inspiration, that, on the contrary, it not only of its very nature precludes the presence of error, but as necessarily excludes it and forbids it as God, the Supreme Truth, necessarily cannot be the Author of error."

[1] *Ep.* lvii. 9.   [2] *Inter Epp. S. Hier.* cxvi. 3.

Then, after giving the definitions of the Councils of Florence and Trent, confirmed by the Council of the Vatican, Pope Leo continues :

" Consequently it is not to the point to suggest that the Holy Spirit used men as His instruments for writing, and that therefore, while no error is referable to the primary Author, it may well be due to the inspired authors themselves. For by supernatural power the Holy Spirit so stirred them and moved them to write, so stood by them as they wrote, that their minds could rightly conceive only those and all those things which He Himself bade them conceive ; only such things could they faithfully commit to writing and aptly express with unerring truth ; else God would not be the Author of the entirety of Sacred Scripture."[1]

---

[1] *Litt. Encycl.*, " Providentissimus Deus."

C

How certain Modern Views compare with this Teaching

(a) THERE ARE NO SUCH THINGS AS "PRIMARY AND SECONDARY ELEMENTS" IN THE BIBLE

BUT although these words of our predecessor leave no room for doubt or dispute, it grieves us to find that not only men outside, but even children of the Catholic Church—nay, what is a peculiar sorrow to us, even clerics and professors of sacred learning—who in their own conceit either openly repudiate or at least attack in secret the Church's teaching on this point.

We warmly commend, of course, those who, with the assistance of critical methods, seek to discover new ways of explaining the difficulties in Holy Scripture, whether for their own guidance or to help others. But we remind them that they will only come to miserable grief if they neglect our predecessor's injunctions and overstep the limits set by the Fathers.

Yet no one can pretend that certain recent writers really adhere to these limitations. For while conceding that inspiration extends to every phrase—and, ·indeed, to every single word of Scripture—yet, by endeavouring to distinguish between what they style the primary or religious and the secondary or profane element in the Bible, they claim that the effect of inspiration—namely, absolute truth and immunity from error—are to be restricted to that primary or religious element. Their notion is that only what concerns religion is intended and taught by God in Scripture, and that all the rest— things concerning " profane knowledge," the garments in which Divine truth is presented—God merely permits, and even leaves to the individual author's greater or less knowledge. Small wonder, then, that in their view a considerable number of things occur in the Bible touching physical science, history and the like, which cannot be reconciled with modern progress in science !

Some even maintain that these views do not conflict with what our predecessor laid down since—so they claim— he said that the sacred writers spoke in accordance with the external—and thus deceptive—appearance of things in nature. But the Pontiff's own words show that this is a rash and false deduction. For sound philosophy teaches that the senses can never be deceived as regards their own proper and immediate object. Therefore, from the merely external appearances of things—of which, of course, we have always to take account as Leo XIII., following in the footsteps of St. Augustine and St. Thomas, most wisely remarks—we can never conclude that there is any error in Sacred Scripture.

Moreover, our predecessor, sweeping aside all such distinctions between what these critics are pleased to call primary and secondary elements, says in no ambiguous fashion that " those who fancy that when it is a question of the truth of certain expressions we have not got to consider so much what God said as why He said it," are very far indeed from the truth. He also teaches that Divine inspiration extends to every part of the

Bible without the slightest exception, and that no error can occur in the inspired text :

" It would be wholly impious to limit inspiration to certain portions only of Scripture or to concede that the sacred authors themselves could have erred."

(*b*) NOR CAN WE ALLOW OF A " RELATIVE FORM OF TRUTH " IN IT

Those, too, who hold that the historical portions of Scripture do not rest on the absolute truth of the facts but merely upon what they are pleased to term their relative truth, namely, what people then commonly thought, are—no less than are the aforementioned critics —out of harmony with the Church's teaching, which is endorsed by the testimony of Jerome and other Fathers. Yet they are not afraid to deduce such views from the words of Leo XIII. on the ground that he allowed that the principles he had laid down touching the things of nature could be applied to historical things as well. Hence they maintain that precisely as the sacred writers spoke of physical things according to appearances, so, too, while ignorant of the facts, they narrated them in accordance with general opinion or even on baseless evidence ; neither do they tell us the sources whence they derived their knowledge, nor do they make other peoples' narrative their own. Such views are clearly false, and constitute a calumny on our predecessor. After all, what analogy is there between physics and history ? For whereas physics are concerned with " sensible appearances " and must consequently square with phenomena, history on the contrary, must square with facts,

since history is the written account of events as they
actually occurred.   If we were to accept such views,
how could we maintain the truth insisted on throughout
Leo XIII.'s Encyclical—viz. that the sacred narrative
is absolutely free from error ?

And if Leo XIII. does say that we can apply to
history and cognate subjects the same principles which
hold good for science, he yet does not lay this down
as a universal law, but simply says that we can apply
a like line of argument when refuting the fallacies of
adversaries and defending the historical truth of Scripture
from their assaults.

(c) IS THE BIBLE GENUINE HISTORY ?

Nor do modern innovators stop here : they even try to
claim St. Jerome as a patron of their views on the ground
that he maintained that historic truth and sequence were
not observed in the Bible, " precisely as things actually
took place, but in accordance with what men thought at
that time," and that he even held that this was the true
norm for history.[1]   A strange distortion of St. Jerome's
words !   He does not say that when giving us an account
of events the writer was ignorant of the truth and simply
adopted the false views then current ; he merely says that
in giving names to persons or things he followed general
custom.   Thus the Evangelist calls St. Joseph the father
of Jesus, but what he meant by the title " father " here is
abundantly clear from the whole context.   For St. Jerome
" the true norm of history " is this : when it is question
of such appellatives (as " father," etc.), and when there is

[1] *In* Jer. xxviii. 10 ss. ; *in* Matt. xiv. 8 ; *Adv. Helvid.* 4.

no danger of error, then a writer must adopt the ordinary forms of speech simply because such forms of speech are in ordinary use. More than this: Jerome maintains that belief in the Biblical narrative is as necessary to salvation as is belief in the doctrines of the faith ; thus in his Commentary on the Epistle to Philemon he says:

" What I mean is this: Does any man believe in God the Creator? He cannot do so unless he first believe that the things written of God's Saints are true." He then gives examples from the Old Testament, and adds : " Now unless a man believes all these and other things too which are written of the Saints he cannot believe in the God of the Saints."[1]

Thus St. Jerome is in complete agreement with St. Augustine, who sums up the general belief of Christian antiquity when he says:

" Holy Scripture is invested with supreme authority by reason of its sure and momentous teachings regarding the faith. Whatever, then, it tells us of Enoch, Elias and Moses—that we believe. We do not, for instance, believe that God's Son was born of the Virgin Mary simply because He could not otherwise have appeared in the flesh and ' walked amongst men '—as Faustus would have it—but we believe it simply because it is written in Scripture ; and unless we believe in Scripture we can neither be Christians nor be saved."[2]

(d) NEITHER CAN WE ADMIT THE THEORY OF SO-CALLED " TACIT QUOTATIONS "

Then there are other assailants of Holy Scripture who misuse principles—which are only sound if kept within

---

[1] *In* Phil. iv.   [2] *Contra Faustum* xxvi. 3, 6.

due bounds—in order to overturn the fundamental truth
of the Bible and thus destroy Catholic teaching handed
down by the Fathers.   If Jerome were living now he
would sharpen his keenest controversial weapons against
people who set aside what is the mind and judgment of
the Church, and take too ready a refuge in such notions
as "implicit quotations" or "pseudo-historical narratives,"
or in "kinds of literature" in the Bible such as cannot be
reconciled with the entire and perfect truth of God's
word, or who suggest such origins of the Bible as must
inevitably weaken—if not destroy—its authority.   What
can we say of men who in expounding the very Gospels
so whittle away the human trust we should repose in it as
to overturn Divine faith in it?   They refuse to allow that
the things which Christ said or did have come down to us
unchanged and entire through witnesses who carefully
committed to writing what they themselves had seen or
heard.   They maintain—and particularly in their treatment of the *Fourth Gospel*—that much is due of course to
the Evangelists—who, however, added much from their
own imaginations ; but much, too, is due to narratives com-
piled by the faithful at other periods, the result, of course,
being that the twin streams now flowing in the same
channel cannot be distinguished from one another.   Not
thus did Jerome and Augustine and the other Doctors of
the Church understand the historical trustworthiness of
the Gospels ; yet of it one wrote : "He that saw it hath
given testimony, and his testimony is true.   And he
knoweth that he saith true that you also may believe."[1] So,
too, St. Jerome : after rebuking the heretical framers of

[1] John xix. 35.

the apocryphal Gospels for "attempting rather to fill up the story than to tell it truly,"[1] he says of the Canonical Scriptures : "None can doubt but that what is written took place."[2] Here again he is in fullest harmony with Augustine, who so beautifully says :

"These things are true ; they are faithfully and truth-fully written of Christ ; so that whosoever believes His Gospel may be thereby instructed in the truth and misled by no lie."[3]

(*e*) NONE OF THESE NOTIONS ARE COMPATIBLE WITH TRADITIONAL VIEWS ON THE BIBLE, NOR INDEED WITH CHRIST'S OWN METHOD OF EMPLOYING IT

All this shows us how earnestly we must strive to avoid, as children of the Church, this insane freedom in venti-lating opinions which the Fathers were careful to shun. This we shall more readily achieve if you, Venerable Brethren, will make both clergy and laity committed to your care by the Holy Spirit realise that neither Jerome nor the other Fathers of the Church learned their doctrine touching Holy Scripture save in the school of the Divine Master Himself. We know what He felt about Holy Scripture : when He said, "It is written," and "the Scrip-ture must needs be fulfilled," we have therein an argument which admits of no exception and which should put an end to all controversy. Yet it is worth while dwelling on this point a little : when Christ preached to the people, whether on the Mount by the lake-side, or in the syna-gogue at Nazareth, or in His own city of Capharnaum,

---

[1] *Prol. in Comment. in* Matt.
[2] *Ep.* lxxviii. 1.   [3] *Contra Faustum* xxvi. 8.

He took His points and His arguments from the Bible. From the same source came His weapons when disputing with the Scribes and Pharisees. Whether teaching or disputing He quotes from all parts of Scripture and takes his examples from it ; He quotes it as an argument which must be accepted. He refers without any discrimination of sources to the stories of Jonas and the Ninivites, of the Queen of Sheba and Solomon, of Elias and Eliseus, of David and of Noe, of Lot and the Sodomites, and even of Lot's wife.[1] How solemn His witness to the truth of the sacred books : " One jot, or one tittle shall not pass of the Law till all be fulfilled ";[2] and again : " The Scripture cannot be broken ";[3] and consequently : " He therefore that shall break one of these least commandments, and shall so teach men shall be called the least in the kingdom of heaven."[4] Before His Ascension, too, when He would steep His Apostles in the same doctrine: " He opened their understanding that they might understand the Scriptures. And He said to them : thus it is written, and thus it behoved Christ to suffer, and to rise again from the dead the third day."[5] In a word, then : Jerome's teaching on the superexcellence and truth of Scripture is Christ's teaching. Wherefore we exhort all the Church's children, and especially those whose duty it is to teach in seminaries, to follow closely in St. Jerome's footsteps. If they will but do so they will learn to prize as he prized the treasure of the Scriptures, and will derive from them most abundant and blessed fruit.

[1] *Cf.* Matt. xii. 3, 39-42; Luke xvii. 26-29, 32.
[2] Matt. v. 18.   [3] John x. 35.
[4] Matt. v. 19.   [5] Luke xxiv. 45

D

How to Study the Bible

NOW, if we make use of the "Greatest of Doctors" as our guide and teacher we shall derive from so doing not only the gains signalised above, but others too, which cannot be regarded as trifling or few. What these gains are, Venerable Brethren, we will set out briefly. At the outset, then, we are deeply impressed by the intense love of the Bible which St. Jerome exhibits in his whole life and teaching : both are steeped in the Spirit of God. This intense love of the Bible he was ever striving to kindle in the hearts of the faithful, and his words on this subject to the maiden Demetrias are really addressed to us all :

" Love the Bible and wisdom will love you ; love it and it will preserve you ; honour it and it will embrace you ; these are the jewels which you should wear on your breast and in your ears."[1]

His unceasing reading of the Bible and his painstaking study of each book—nay, of every phrase and word—gave him a knowledge of the text such as no other ecclesiastical writer of old possessed. It is due to this

---

[1] *Ep.* cxxx 20

familiarity with the text and to his own acute judgment that the Vulgate version Jerome made is, in the judgment of all capable men, preferable to any other ancient version, since it appears to give us the sense of the original more accurately and with greater elegance than they. The said Vulgate, "approved by so many centuries of use in the Church," was pronounced by the Council of Trent "authentic," and the same Council insisted that it was to be used in teaching and in the liturgy. If God in His mercy grants us life, we sincerely hope to see an amended and faithfully restored edition. We have no doubt that when this arduous task—entrusted by our predecessor, Pius X., to the Benedictine Order—has been completed it will prove of great assistance in the study of the Bible.

But to return to St. Jerome's love of the Bible : this is so conspicuous in his letters that they almost seem woven out of Scripture texts ; and, as St. Bernard found no taste in things which did not echo the most sweet Name of Jesus, so no literature made any appeal to Jerome unless it derived its light from Holy Scripture. Thus he wrote to Paulinus, formerly senator and even consul, and only recently converted to the faith :

" If only you had this foundation (knowledge of Scripture) ; nay, more—if you would but let Scripture give the finishing touches to your work—I should find nothing more beautiful, more learned, even nothing more Latin than your volumes. . . . If you could but add to your wisdom and eloquence study of and real acquaintance with Holy Scripture, we should speedily have to acknowledge you a leader amongst us."[1]

[1] *Ep.* lviii. 9, 11.

How we are to seek for this great treasure, given as it is by our Father in heaven for our solace during this earthly pilgrimage, St. Jerome's example shows us. First, we must be well prepared and must possess a good will. Thus Jerome himself, immediately on his baptism, determined to remove whatever might prove a hindrance to his ambitions in this respect. Like the man who found a treasure and "for joy thereof went and sold all that he had and bought that field,"[1] so did Jerome say farewell to the idle pleasures of this passing world ; he went into the desert, and since he realised what risks he had run in the past through the allurements of vice, he adopted a most severe style of life. With all obstacles thus removed he prepared his soul for "the knowledge of Jesus Christ" and for putting on Him Who was "meek and humble of heart." But he went through what Augustine also experienced when he took up the study of Scripture. For the latter has told us how, steeped as a youth in Cicero and profane authors, the Bible "seemed to me unfit to be compared with Cicero. My swelling pride shrank from its modest garb, while my gaze could not pierce to what the latter hid. Of a truth Scripture was meant to grow up with the childlike ; but then I could not be childlike; turgid eloquence appealed mightily to me."[2] So, too, St. Jerome ; even though withdrawn into the desert he still found such delight in profane literature that at first he failed to discern the lowly Christ in His lowly Scriptures :

"Wretch that I was ! I read Cicero even before I broke my fast ! And after the long night-watches, when

---

[1] Matt. xiii. 44. [2] *Confessions* iii. 5; *cf.* viii. 12.

memory of my past sins wrung tears from my soul, even
then I took up my Plautus! Then perhaps I would come
to my senses and would start reading the Prophets. But
their uncouth language made me shiver, and, since blind
eyes do not see the light, I blamed the sun and not my
own eyes."[1]

But in a brief space Jerome became so enamoured of
the "folly of the Cross" that he himself serves as a proof
of the extent to which a humble and devout frame of
mind is conducive to the understanding of Holy Scripture. He realised that "in expounding Scripture we
need God's Holy Spirit";[2] he saw that one cannot
otherwise read or understand it "than the Holy Spirit
by Whom it was written demands."[3]   Consequently, he
was ever humbly praying for God's assistance and for the
light of the Holy Spirit, and asking his friends to do the
same for him.   We find him commending to the Divine
assistance and to his brethren's prayers his Commentaries
on various books as he began them, and then rendering
God due thanks when completed.

(b) HE ALSO SHOWS US THE NEED OF A LIVELY CATHOLIC FAITH

As he trusted to God's grace, so too did he rely upon
the authority of his predecessors : "What I have learned
I did not teach myself—a wretchedly presumptuous
teacher !—but I learned it from illustrious men in the
Church."[4]   Again : "In studying Scripture I never

[1] *Ep.* xxii. 30.   [2] *In* Mich. i. 10, 15.
[3] *In* Gal. v. 19.   [4] *Ep.* cviii. 26.

trusted to myself."[1] To Theophilus, Bishop of Alexandria, he imparted the rule he had laid down for his own student life :

"It has always been my custom to fight for the prerogatives of a Christian, not to overpass the limits set by the Fathers, always to bear in mind that Roman faith praised by the Apostle."[2]

He ever paid submissive homage to the Church, our supreme teacher through the Roman Pontiffs. Thus, with a view to putting an end to the controversy raging in the East concerning the mystery of the Holy Trinity, he submitted the question to the Roman See for settlement, and wrote from the Syrian desert to Pope Damasus as follows :

"I decided, therefore, to consult the Chair of Peter and that Roman faith which the Apostle praised ; I ask for my soul's food from that city wherein I first put on the garment of Christ. . . . I, who follow no other leader save Christ, associate myself with Your Blessedness, in communion, that is, with the Chair of Peter. For I know the Church was built upon that Rock. . . . I beg you to settle this dispute. If you desire it I shall not be afraid to say there are Three Hypostases. If it is your wish let them draw up a Symbol of faith subsequent to that of Nicæa, and let us orthodox praise God in the same form of words as the Arians employ."[3]

And in his next letter : "Meanwhile I keep crying out, 'Any man who is joined to Peter's Chair, he is my man.'"[4] Since he had learnt this "rule of faith" from

[1] *Præfat. in* 1 Paral. [2] *Ep.* lxiii. 2.
[3] *Ep.* xv. 1. [4] *Ep.* xvi. 2.

his study of the Bible, he was able to refute a false interpretation of a Biblical text with the simple remark :
" Yes, but the Church of God does not 'admit that."[1]
When, again, Vigilantius quoted an Apocryphal book,
Jerome was content to reply : " A book I have never so
much as read! For what is the good of soiling one's
hands with a book the Church does not receive?"[2]
With his strong insistence on adhering to the integrity
of the faith, it is not to be wondered at that he attacked
vehemently those who left the Church ; he promptly
regarded them as his own personal enemies.   " To put it
briefly," he says, " I have never spared heretics, and have
always striven to regard the Church's enemies as my
own."[3]   To Rufinus he writes : " There is one point in
which I cannot agree with you : you ask me to spare
heretics—or, in other words—not to prove myself a
Catholic."[4]   Yet at the same time Jerome deplored the
lamentable state of heretics, and adjured them to return
to their sorrowing Mother, the one source of salvation ;[5]
he prayed, too, with all earnestness for the conversion of
those " who had quitted the Church and put away the
Holy Spirit's teaching to follow their own notions."[6]

Was there ever a time, Venerable Brethren, when there
was greater call than now for us all, lay and cleric alike,
to imbibe the spirit of this " Greatest of Doctors " ?
For there are many contumacious folk now who sneer at
the authority and government of God, Who has revealed

---

[1] In Dan. iii. 37.   [2] Adv. Vigil. 6.
[3] Dial. contra Pelagianos, Prol. ii.
[4] Contra Rufin. iii. 43.
[5] In Mich. i. 10.   [6] In Isa. xvi. 1-5.

Himself and of the Church which teaches. You know
—for Leo XIII. warned us—"how insistently men fight
against us; you know the arms and arts they rely upon."
It is your duty, then, to train as many really fit defenders
of this holiest of causes as you can. They must be ready
to combat not only those who deny the existence of
the Supernatural Order altogether, and are thus led to
deny the existence of any divine revelation or inspiration,
but those, too, who—through an itching desire for novelty
—venture to interpret the sacred books as though they
were of purely human origin; those, too, who scoff at
opinions held of old in the Church, or who, through
contempt of its teaching office, either reck little of, or
silently disregard, or at least obstinately endeavour to
adapt to their own views, the Constitutions of the
Apostolic See or the decisions of the Pontifical Biblical
Commission.

Would that all Catholics would cling to St. Jerome's
golden rule and obediently listen to their Mother's words,
so as modestly to keep within the bounds marked out by
the Fathers and ratified by the Church.

To return, however, to the question of the formation
of Biblical students. We must lay the foundations in
piety and humility of mind; only when we have done
that does St. Jerome invite us to study the Bible. In
the first place, he insists, in season and out, on daily
reading of the text. "Provided," he says, "our bodies
are not the slaves of sin, wisdom will come to us; but
exercise your mind, feed it daily with Holy Scripture."[1]
And again :

[1] *Comment.* on Tit. iii. 9.

" We have got, then, to read Holy Scripture assiduously ; we have got to meditate on the Law of God day
and night so that, as expert money-changers, we may be
able to detect false coin from true."[1]

For matrons and maidens alike he lays down the same
rule. Thus, writing to the Roman matron Laeta about
her daughter's training, he says :

" Every day she should give you a definite account of
her Bible-reading. . . . For her the Bible must take
the place of silks and jewels. . . . Let her learn the
Psalter first, and find her recreation in its songs ; let her
learn from Solomon's Proverbs the way of life, from
Ecclesiastes how to trample on the world. In Job she
will find an example of patient virtue. Thence let her
pass to the Gospels ; they should always be in her hands.
She should steep herself in the Acts and the Epistles.
And when she has enriched her soul with these treasures
she should commit to memory the Prophets, the Hepta-
teuch, Kings and Chronicles, Esdras and Esther ; then
she can learn the Canticle of Canticles without any fear."[2]

He says the same to Eustochium :

" Read assiduously and learn as much as you can.
Let sleep find you holding your Bible, and when your
head nods let it be resting on the sacred page."[3]

When he sent Eustochium the epitaph he had composed
for her mother Paula, he especially praises that holy woman
for having so whole-heartedly devoted herself and her
daughter to Bible study that she knew the Bible through
and through, and had committed it to memory. He
continues :

[1] *Comment.* on Eph. iv. 31.   [2] *Ep.* cvii. 9.
[3] *Ep.* xxii. 17, 29.

" I will tell you another thing about her, though evil-disposed people may cavil at it : she determined to learn Hebrew, a language which I myself, with immense labour and toil from my youth upwards, have only partly learned, and which I even now dare not cease studying lest it should quit me. But Paula learned it, and so well that she could chant the Psalms in Hebrew, and could speak it, too, without any trace of a Latin accent. We can see the same thing even now in her daughter Eustochium."[1]

He tells us much the same of Marcella, who also knew the Bible exceedingly well.[2] And none can fail to see what profit and sweet tranquillity must result in well-disposed souls from such devout reading of the Bible. Whosoever comes to it in piety, faith and humility, and with a determination to make progress in it, will assuredly find therein and will eat the " Bread that cometh down from heaven " ; he will, in his own person, experience the truth of David's words : " The hidden and uncertain things of Thy Wisdom Thou hast made manifest to me !" For this table of the " Divine Word " does really " contain holy teaching, teach the true faith, and lead us unfalteringly beyond the veil into the Holy of holies."[3]

Hence, as far as in us lies, we, Venerable Brethren, shall, with St. Jerome as our guide, never desist from urging the faithful to read daily the Gospels, the Acts and the Epistles, so as to gather thence food for their souls.

Our thoughts naturally turn just now to the Society of St. Jerome, which we ourselves were instrumental in

---

[1] *Ep.* cviii. 26.   [2] *Ep.* cxxvii. 7.
[3] *Imitatio Christi* iv. 11.

founding ; its success has gladdened us, and we trust that the future will see a great impulse given to it.

The object of this Society is to put into the hands of as many people as possible the Gospels and Acts, so that every Christian family may have them and become accustomed to reading them. This we have much at heart, for we have seen how useful it is. We earnestly hope, then, that similar Societies will be founded in your dioceses and affiliated to the parent Society here.

Commendation, too, is due to Catholics in other countries who have published the entire New Testament, as well as selected portions of the Old, in neat and simple form so as to popularise their use. Much gain must accrue to the Church of God when numbers of people thus approach this table of heavenly instruction which the Lord provided through the ministry of His Prophets, Apostles and Doctors, for the entire Christian world.

E

The Part the Bible must play in Priestly Education

(a) THE NEED OF BIBLICAL LEARNING

IF, then, St. Jerome begs for assiduous reading of the Bible by the faithful in general, he insists on it for those who are called to "bear the yoke of Christ" and preach His word. His words to Rusticus the monk apply to all clerics :

"So long as you are in your own country regard your cell as your orchard; there you can gather Scripture's various fruits and enjoy the pleasures it affords you. Always have a book in your hands—and read it ; learn the Psalter by heart ; pray unceasingly ; watch over your · senses lest idle thoughts creep in."[1]

Similarly to Nepotian :

"Constantly read the Bible ; in fact, have it always in your hands. Learn what you have got to teach. Get firm hold of that 'faithful word that is according to doctrine, that you may be able to exhort in sound doctrine and convince the gainsayers.' "[2]

When reminding Paulinus of the lessons St. Paul gave to Timothy and Titus, and which he himself had derived from the Bible, Jerome says :

"A mere holy rusticity only avails the man himself ; but however much a life so meritorious may serve to build

[1] *Ep.* cxxvii. 7, 11.   [2] *Ep.* lii. 7; *cf.* Tit. i. 9.

up the Church of God, it does quite as much harm to the
Church if it fails to 'resist the gainsayer.' Malachi the
Prophet says, or rather the Lord says it by Malachi :
'Ask for the Law from the priests.' For it is the priest's
duty to give an answer when asked about the Law. In
Deuteronomy we read : 'Ask thy father and he will tell
thee ; ask the priests and they will tell thee. . . .' Daniel,
too, at the close of his glorious vision, declares that 'the
just shall shine like stars and they that are learned as the
brightness of the firmament.' What a vast difference, then,
between a righteous rusticity and a learned righteousness !
The former likened to the stars ; the latter to the heavens
themselves !" [1]

He writes ironically to Marcella about the "self-
righteous lack of education" noticeable in some clerics,
who

"think that to be without culture and to be holy are the
same thing, and who dub themselves 'disciples of the
fisherman '; as though they were holy simply because
ignorant !"[2]

Nor is it only the "uncultured " whom Jerome condemns.
Learned clerics sin through ignorance of the Bible ; therefore he demands of them an assiduous reading of the text.

(b) OF THE PONTIFICAL BIBLICAL INSTITUTE

Strive, then, Venerable Brethren, to bring home to your
clerics and priests these teachings of the Sainted Commentator. You have to remind them constantly of the
demands made by their divine vocation if they would be
worthy of it : " The lips of the priest shall keep knowledge,
and men shall ask the Law at his mouth, for he is the

---

[1] *Ep.* liii. 3.   [2] *Ep.* xxvii. 1.

Angel of the Lord of hosts."[1] They must realise, then, that they cannot neglect study of the Bible, and that this can only be undertaken along the lines laid down by Leo XIII. in his Encyclical, "Providentissimus Deus." They cannot do this better than by frequenting the Biblical Institute established by our predecessor, Pius X., in accordance with the wishes of Leo XIII. As the experience of the past ten years has shown, it has proved a great gain to the Church. Not all, however, can avail themselves of this. It will be well, then, Venerable Brethren, that picked men, both of the secular and regular clergy, should come to Rome for Biblical study. All will not come with the same object. Some, in accordance with the real purpose of the Institute, will so devote themselves to Biblical study that "afterwards, both in private and in public, whether by writing or by teaching, whether as professors in Catholic schools or by writing in defence of Catholic truth, they may be able worthily to uphold the cause of Biblical study."[2] Others, however, already priests, will obtain here a wider knowledge of the Bible than they were able to acquire during their theological course ; they will gain, too, an acquaintance with the great commentators and with Biblical history and geography. Such knowledge will avail them much in their ministry ; they will be "instructed to every good work."[3]

[1] Mal. ii. 7.
[2] Pius X., *Vinea electa*, May 7, 1909.
[3] 2 Tim. iii. 17.

(c) THE IMMEDIATE GOAL OF OUR STUDY OF THE BIBLE IS OUR OWN SPIRITUAL FORMATION

We learn, then, from St. Jerome's example and teaching the qualities required in one who would devote himself to Biblical study. But what, in his view, is the goal of such study? First, that from the Bible's pages we learn spiritual perfection. Meditating as he did day and night on the Law of the Lord and on His Scriptures, Jerome himself found there the " Bread that cometh down from heaven," the manna containing all delights.[1] And we certainly cannot do without that bread. How can a cleric teach others the way of salvation if through neglect of meditation on God's word he fails to teach himself? What confidence can he have that, when ministering to others, he is really "a leader of the blind, a light to them that are in darkness, an instructor of the foolish, having the form of knowledge and of truth in the law," if he is unwilling to study the said Law and thus shuts the door on any divine illumination on it?

Alas! many of God's ministers, through never looking at their Bible, perish themselves and allow many others to perish also. " The children have asked for bread, and there was none to break it to them ";[2] and " With desolation is all the land made desolate, for there is none that meditateth in the heart."[3]

(d) THE LESS IMMEDIATE GOAL IS THE DEFENCE OF CATHOLIC TRUTH

Secondly, it is from the Bible that we gather confirmations and illustrations of any particular doctrine we wish

[1] *Tract. in* Ps. cxlvii.　　[2] Lam. iv. 4.　　[3] Jer. xii. 11.

to defend. In this Jerome was marvellously expert. When disputing with the heretics of his day he refuted by singularly apt and weighty arguments drawn from the Bible. If men of the present age would but imitate him in this we should see realised what our predecessor, Leo XIII., in his Encyclical, " Providentissimus Deus," said was so eminently desirable : " The Bible influencing our theological teaching and indeed becoming its very soul."

Lastly, the real value of the Bible is for our preaching— if the latter is to be fruitful. On this point it is a pleasure to illustrate from Jerome what we ourselves said in our Encyclical on " preaching the Word of God," entitled *Humani generis*. How insistently Jerome urges on priests assiduous reading of the Bible if they would worthily teach and preach ! Their words will have neither value nor weight nor any power to touch men's souls save in proportion as they are " informed " by Holy Scripture : " Let a priest's speech be seasoned with the Bible,"[1] for " the Scriptures are a trumpet that stirs us with a mighty voice and penetrates to the souls of them that believe,"[2] and " nothing so strikes home as an example taken from the Bible."[3]

(e) FOR THIS PURPOSE ST. JEROME LAYS DOWN CERTAIN RULES OF INTERPRETATION

These mainly concern the exegetes, yet preachers, too, must always bear them in mind. Jerome's first rule is careful study of the actual words so that we may be perfectly certain what the writer really does say. He was most

[1] *Ep.* lii. 8.   [2] *In* Amos iii. 3.   [3] *In* Zach. ix. 15.

careful to consult the original text, to compare various versions, and, if he discovered any mistake in them, to explain it and thus make the text perfectly clear. The precise meaning, too, that attaches to particular words has to be worked out, for "when discussing Holy Scripture it is not words we want so much as the meaning of words."[1] We do not for a moment deny that Jerome, in imitation of Latin and Greek doctors before him, leaned too much, especially at the outset, towards allegorical interpretations. But his love of the Bible, his unceasing toil in reading and re-reading it and weighing its meaning, compelled him to an ever-growing appreciation of its literal sense and to the formulation of sound principles regarding it. These we set down here, for they mark out a safe path for us if we would discover the Bible's meaning.

In the first place, then, we must study the literal or historical meaning :

"I earnestly warn the prudent reader not to pay attention to superstitious interpretations such as are given cut and dried according to some interpreter's fancy. He should study the beginning, middle, and end, and so form a connected idea of the whole of what he finds written."[2]

Jerome then goes on to say that all interpretation rests on the literal sense,[3] and that we are not to think that there is no literal sense merely because a thing is said metaphorically, for "the history itself is often presented in metaphorical dress and described figuratively."[4] Indeed,

[1] *Ep.* xxix. 1.   [2] *In* Matt. xxv. 13.
[3] *Cf. in* Ezech. xxxviii. 1; xli. 23; *in* Marc. i. 13-31; *Ep.* cxxix. 6.
[4] *In* Hab. iii. 14.

he himself affords the best refutation of those who maintain that he says that certain passages have no historical meaning : " We are not rejecting the history, we are merely giving a spiritual interpretation of it."[1] Once, however, he has firmly established the literal or historical meaning, Jerome goes on to seek out deeper and hidden meanings, so as to nourish his mind with more delicate food. Thus he says of the Book of Proverbs—and he makes the same remark about other parts of the Bible— that we must not stop at the simple literal sense :

" Just as we have to seek gold in the earth, for the kernel in the shell, for the chestnut's hidden fruit beneath its hairy coverings, so in Holy Scripture we have to dig deep for its divine meaning."[2]

When teaching Paulinus " how to make true progress in the Bible," he says :

" Everything we read in the Sacred Books shines and glitters even in its outer shell ; but the marrow of it is sweeter. If you want the kernel you must break the shell."[3]

At the same time, he insists that in searching for this deeper meaning we must proceed in due order, " lest in our search for spiritual riches we seem to despise the history as poverty-stricken."[4] Consequently he repudiates many mystical interpretations alleged by ancient writers ; for he feels that they are not sufficiently based on the literal meaning :

[1] *In* Mark ix. 1-7 ; *cf. in* Ezech. xl. 24-27.
[2] *In* Eccles. xii. 9. [3] *Ep.* lix. 9.
[4] *In* Eccles. ii. 24.

" When all these promises of which the Prophets sang
are regarded not merely as empty sounds or idle tropo-
logical expressions, but as stablished on earth and having
solid historical foundations, then, and only then, can we
put on them the coping-stone of a spiritual interpretation."[1]

On this point he makes the wise remark that we ought
not to desert the path mapped out by Christ and His
Apostles, who, while regarding the Old Testament as
preparing for and foreshadowing the New Covenant, and
whilst consequently explaining various passages in the
former as figurative, yet do not give a figurative interpretation of all alike.   In confirmation of this he often refers
us to St. Paul, who, when

" explaining the mystery of Adam and Eve, did not
deny that they were formed, but on that historical basis
erected a spiritual interpretation, and said : ' Therefore
shall a man leave,' etc."[2]

(f) IN WHAT TRUE PULPIT ELOQUENCE CONSISTS

If only Biblical students and preachers would but
follow this example of Christ and His Apostles ; if they
would but obey the directions of Leo XIII., and not
neglect " those allegorical or similar explanations which
the Fathers have given, especially when these are based
on the literal sense, and are supported by weighty
authority"; if they would pass from the literal to the
more profound meaning in temperate fashion, and thus
lift themselves to a higher plane, they would, with St.
Jerome, realise how true are St. Paul's words : " All

[1] *In* Amos ix. 6.   [2] *In* Isa. vi. 1-7.

Scripture inspired of God is profitable to teach, to reprove, to correct, to instruct in justice." [1]

They would, too, derive abundant help from the infinite treasury of facts and ideas in the Bible, and would thence be able to mould firmly but gently the lives and characters of the faithful.

As for methods of expounding Holy Scripture—"for amongst the dispensers of the mysteries of God it is required that a man be found faithful "—St. Jerome lays down that we have got to keep to the

" true interpretation, and that the real function of a commentator is to set forth not what he himself would like his author to mean, but what he really does mean." [2]

And he continues :

" It is dangerous to speak in the Church, lest through some faulty interpretation we make Christ's Gospel into man's Gospel." [3]

And again :

" In explaining the Bible we need no florid oratorical composition, but that learned simplicity which is truth." [4]

This ideal he ever kept before him ; he acknowledges that in his Commentaries he " seeks no praise, but so to set out what another has well said that it may be understood in the sense in which it was said." [5] He further demands of an expositor of Scripture a style which,

" while leaving no impression of haziness . . . yet explains things, sets out the meaning, clears up obscurities, and is not mere verbiage." [6]

[1] 2 Tim. iii. 16. [2] *Ep.* xlix. (xlviii.) 17.
[3] *In* Gal. i. 11. [4] *Præf. in* Amos.
[5] *Præf. in* Gal. [6] *Ep.* xxxvi. 14; *cf.* cxl. 1.

And here we may set down some passages from his writings which will serve to show to what an extent he shrank from that declamatory kind of eloquence which simply aims at winning empty applause by an equally empty and noisy flow of words. He says to Nepotian:

" I do not 'want you to be a declaimer or a garrulous brawler; rather be skilled in the Mysteries, learned in the Sacraments of God. To make the populace gape by spinning words and speaking like a whirlwind is only worthy of empty-headed men."[1]

And once more :

"Students ordained at this time seem not to think how they may get at the real marrow of Holy Scripture, but how best they may make peoples' ears tingle by their flowery declamations !"[2]

Again :

" I prefer to say nothing of men who, like myself, have passed from profane literature to Biblical study, but who, if they happen once to have caught men's ears by their ornate sermons, straightway begin to fancy that whatsoever they say is God's law. Apparently they do not think it worth while to discover what the Prophets and Apostles really meant ; they are content to string together texts made to fit the meaning they want. One would almost fancy that instead of being a degraded species of oratory, it must be a fine thing to pervert the meaning of the text and compel the reluctant Scripture to yield the meaning one wants!"[3]

---

[1] *Ep.* lii. 8.
[2] *Dialogus contra Luciferianos* xi.
[3] *Ep.* liii. 7.

" As a matter of fact, mere loquacity would not win any credit unless backed by Scriptural authority, when, that is, men see that the speaker is trying to give his false doctrine Biblical support."[1]

Moreover, this garrulous eloquence and wordy rusticity

"lacks biting power, has nothing vivid or life-giving in it ; it is flaccid, languid and enervated ; it is like boiled herbs and grass, which speedily dry up and wither away."

On the contrary the Gospel teaching is straightforward, it is like that "least of all seeds"—the mustard seed—"no mere vegetable, but something that 'grows into a tree so that the birds of the air come and dwell in its branches.' "[2] The consequence is that everybody hears gladly this simple and holy fashion of speech, for it is clear and has real beauty without artificiality :

" There are certain eloquent folk who puff out their cheeks and produce a foaming torrent of words ; may they win all the eulogiums they crave for ! For myself, I prefer so to speak that I may be intelligible ; when I discuss the Bible I prefer the Bible's simplicity. . . .[3] ' A cleric's exposition of the Bible should, of course, have a certain becoming eloquence ; but he must keep this in the background, for he must ever have in view the human race and not the leisurely philosophical schools with their choice coterie of disciples.' "[4]

[1] Tit. i. 10.
[2] *Comment. in* Matt. xiii. 32.
[3] *Ep.* xxxvi. 14.
[4] *Ep.* xlviii. (xlix.) 4.

If the younger clergy would but strive to reduce principles like these to practice, and if their elders would keep such principles before their eyes, we are well assured that they would prove of very real assistance to those to whom they minister.

F

The Ultimate Goal of Biblical Study

IN THE BIBLE WE SHALL DISCOVER THE SOUL'S
TRUE DELIGHTS. IN IT WE SHALL ALSO
DISCOVER THE CHURCH. WE SHALL THEN
LEARN WITH ST. JEROME WHAT IT IS TO
LABOUR FOR LOVE OF CHRIST

IT only remains for us, Venerable Brethren, to refer to
those " sweet fruits " which Jerome gathered from
" the bitter seed " of literature. For we confidently
hope that his example will fire both clergy and laity
with enthusiasm for the study of the Bible. It will
be better, however, for you to gather from the lips
of the saintly hermit rather than from our words what
real spiritual delight he found in the Bible and its study.
Notice, then, in what strain he writes to Paulinus, " my
companion, friend, and fellow-mystic ":

" I beseech you to live amidst these things. To
meditate on them, to know nought else, to have no other
interests, this is really a foretaste of the joys of heaven."[1]

He says much the same to his pupil Paula :

" Tell me whether you know of anything more sacred
than this sacred mystery, anything more delightful than the
pleasure found herein ? What food, what honey could be
sweeter than to learn of God's Providence, to enter into His

[1] *Ep.* liii. 10.

shrine and look into the mind of the Creator, to listen to
the Lord's words at which the wise of this world laugh,
but which really are full of spiritual teaching ?   Others
may have their wealth, may drink out of jewelled cups,
be clad in silks, enjoy popular applause, find it impossible
to exhaust their wealth by dissipating it in pleasures of
all kinds ; but our delight is to meditate on the Law
of the Lord day and night, to knock at His door when
shut, to receive our food from the Trinity of Persons,
and, under the guidance of the Lord, trample under foot
the swelling tumults of this world."[1]

And in his Commentary on the Epistle to the Ephesians,
which he dedicated to Paula and her daughter Eustochium,
he says :

" If aught could induce a wise man to cling to this life
or help him to preserve his equanimity amid the conflicts
of the world, it is, I reckon, meditation on and knowledge
of the Bible."[2]

And so it was with Jerome himself: afflicted with
many mental anxieties and bodily pains, he yet ever
enjoyed an interior peace.   Nor was this due simply
to some idle pleasure he found in such studies : it sprang
from love of God and it worked itself out in an earnest
love of God's Church—the divinely appointed guardian
of God's Word.   For in the Books of both Testaments
Jerome saw the Church of God foretold.   Did not
practically every one of the illustrious and sainted women
who hold place of honour in the Old Testament prefigure
the Church, God's Spouse?   Did not the priesthood,
the sacrifices, the solemnities, nay, nearly everything

[1] *Ep.* xxx. 13.   [2] *Prol. in* Eph.

described in the Old Testament, shadow forth that same Church ? How many Psalms and Prophecies he saw fulfilled in that Church ? To him it was clear that the Church's greatest privileges were set forth by Christ and His Apostles. Small wonder, then, that growing familiarity with the Bible meant for Jerome growing love of the Spouse of Christ. We have seen with what reverent yet enthusiastic love he attached himself to the Roman Church and to the See of Peter, how eagerly he attacked those who assailed her. So when applauding Augustine, his junior yet his fellow-soldier, and rejoicing in the fact that they were one in their hatred of heresy, he hails him with the words :

"Well done ! You are famous throughout the world. Catholics revere you and point you out as the stablisher of the old-time faith ; and—an even greater glory—all heretics hate you. And they hate me too ; unable to slay us with the sword they would that wishes could kill."[1]

Sulpicius Severus quotes Postumianus to the same effect :

" His unceasing conflict with wicked men brings on him their hatred. Heretics hate him, for he never ceases attacking them ; clerics hate him, for he assails their criminal lives. But all good men admire him and love him."[2]

And Jerome had to endure much from heretics and abandoned men, especially when the Pelagians laid waste the monastery at Bethlehem. Yet all this he bore with equanimity, like a man who would not hesitate to die for the faith :

" I rejoice when I hear that my children are fighting for Christ. May He in whom we believe confirm our

[1] *Ep.* cxli. 2.   [2] *Dial.* i. 9.

zeal so that we may gladly shed our blood for His faith. Our very home is—as far as worldly belongings go—completely ruined by the heretics ; yet through Christ's mercy it is filled with spiritual riches.   It is better to have to be content with dry bread than to lose one's faith."[1]

And while he never suffered errors to creep in un-noticed, he likewise never failed to lash with biting tongue any looseness in morals, for he was always anxious " to present," unto Christ " a glorious Church, not having spot or wrinkle or any such thing, but that it should be holy and without blemish."[2]   How terribly he upbraids men who have degraded the dignity of the priesthood ! With what vigour he inveighs against the pagan morals then infecting Rome !   But he rightly felt that nothing could better avail to stem this flood of vice than the spectacle afforded by the real beauty of the Christian life ; and that a love of what is really good is the best antidote to evil.   Hence he urged that young people must be piously brought up, the married taught a holy integrity of life, pure souls have the beauty of virginity put before them, that the sweet austerity of an interior life should be extolled, and since the primal law of Christian religion was the combination of toil with charity, that if this could only be preserved human society would recover from its disturbed state.   Of this charity he says very beautifully :

" The believing soul is Christ's true temple.   Adorn it, deck it out, offer your gifts to it, in it receive Christ. Of what profit to have your walls glittering with jewels while Christ dies of hunger in poverty ?"[3]

[1] *Ep.* cxxxix.   [2] Eph. v. 27.   [3] *Ep.* lviii. 7.

As for toil, his whole life and not merely his writings afford the best example. Postumianus, who spent six months with him at Bethlehem, says : " He is wholly occupied in reading and with books ; he rests neither day nor night; he is always either reading or writing something."[1] Jerome's love of the Church, too, shines out even in his Commentaries wherein he lets slip no opportunity for praising the Spouse of Christ:

" The choicest things of all the nations have come and the Lord's House is filled with glory : that is, 'the Church of the Living God, the pillar and the ground of truth.' . . . With jewels like these is the Church richer than ever was the synagogue ; with these living stones is the House of God built up and eternal peace bestowed upon her."[2]

" Come, let us go up to the Mount of the Lord : for we must needs go up if we would come to Christ and to the House of the God of Jacob, to the Church which is ' the pillar and ground of truth.' "[3]

" By the Lord's voice is the Church stablished upon the rock, and her hath the King brought into His chamber, to her by secret condescension hath He put forth His hand through the lattices."[4]

Again and again, as in the passages just given, does Jerome celebrate the intimate union between Christ and His Church. For since the Head can never be separated from the mystical body, so, too, love of Christ is ever associated with zeal for His Church ; and this love of Christ must ever be the chiefest and most agreeable result of a knowledge of Holy Scripture. So convinced indeed

---

[1] Sulpicius Severus, *Dial.* i. 9.
[2] *In* Agg. ii. 1.   [3] *In* Mich. iv. 1.
[4] *Prol. in Comment. in* Matt.

was Jerome that familiarity with the Bible was the royal road to the knowledge and love of Christ that he did not hesitate to say : " Ignorance of the Bible means ignorance of Christ."[1]   And "what other life can there be without knowledge of the Bible wherein Christ, the life of them that believe, is set before us?"[2]   Every single page of either Testament seems to centre round Christ ; hence Jerome, commenting on the words of the Apocalypse about the river and the Tree of Life, says:

" One stream flows out from the throne of God, and that is the Grace of the Holy Spirit, and that grace of the Holy Spirit is in the Holy Scriptures, that is in the stream of the Scriptures.   Yet has that stream twin banks, the Old Testament and the New, and the Tree planted on either side is Christ."[3]

Small wonder, then, if in his devout meditations he applied everything he read in the Bible to Christ:

" When I read the Gospel and find there testimonies from the Law and from the Prophets, I see only Christ ; I so see Moses and the Prophets that I understand them of Christ.   Then when I come to the splendour of Christ Himself, and when I gaze at that glorious sunlight, I care not to look at the lamplight.   For what light can a lamp give when lit in the daytime ?   If the sun shines out the lamplight does not shew.   So, too, when Christ is present the Law and the Prophets do not shew.   Not that I would detract from the Law and the Prophets ; rather do I praise them in that they shew forth Christ. But I so read the Law and the Prophets as not to abide in them but from them to pass to Christ."[4]

---

[1] *Prol. in Comment. in* Isa.; *cf. Tract.* de Ps. lxxvii.
[2] *Ep.* xxx. 7.   [3] *Tract.* de Ps. i.
[4] *Tract. in Marcum* ix. 1-7.

Hence was Jerome wondrously uplifted to love for and knowledge of Christ through his study of the Bible in which he discovered the precious pearl of the Gospel: "There is one most priceless pearl: the knowledge of the Saviour, the mystery of His Passion, the secret of His Resurrection."[1] Burning as he did with the love of Christ, we cannot marvel that, poor and lowly with Christ, with soul freed from earthly cares, he sought Christ alone, by His spirit was he led, with Him he lived in closest intimacy, by imitating Him he would bear about the image of His sufferings in himself. For him nought more glorious than to suffer with and for Christ. Hence it was that when on Damasus' death he left Rome wounded and weary from evil men's assaults, he wrote just before he embarked:

"Though some fancy me a scoundrel and guilty of every crime—and, indeed, this is a small matter when I think of my sins—yet you do well when from your soul you reckon evil men good. Thank God I am deemed worthy to be hated by the world. . . . What real sorrows have I to bear—I who fight for the Cross? Men heap false accusations on me ; yet I know that through ill report and good report we win to the kingdom of heaven."[2]

In like fashion does he exhort the maiden Eustochium to courageous and lifelong toil for Christ's sake:

"To become what the Martyrs, the Apostles, what even Christ Himself was means immense labour—but what a reward ! . . . What I have been saying to you will sound hard to one who does not love Christ. But

[1] *In* Matt. xiii. 45.   [2] *Ep.* xlv. 1.

those who consider worldly pomp a mere offscouring and all under the sun mere nothingness if only they may win Christ, those who are dead with Christ, have risen with Him and have crucified the flesh with its vices and concupiscences—they will echo the words : ' Who shall separate us from the charity of Christ ?' "[1]

Immense, then, was the profit Jerome derived from reading Scripture ; hence came those interior illuminations whereby he was ever more and more drawn to knowledge and love of Christ ; hence, too, that love of prayer of which he has written so well ; hence his wonderful familiarity with Christ, Whose sweetness drew him so that he ran unfalteringly along the arduous way of the Cross to the palm of victory.   Hence, too, his ardent love for the Holy Eucharist : " Who is wealthier than he who carries the Lord's Body in his wicker basket, the Lord's Blood in his crystal vessel ?"[2]   Hence, too, his love for Christ's Mother, whose perpetual virginity he had so keenly defended, whose title as God's Mother and as the greatest example of all the virtues he constantly set before Christ's spouses for their imitation.[3]   No one, then, can wonder that Jerome should have been so powerfully drawn to those spots in Palestine which had been consecrated by the presence of our Redeemer and His Mother. It is easy to recognise the hand of Jerome in the words written from Bethlehem to Marcella by his disciples, Paula and Eustochium :

" What words can serve to describe to you the Saviour's cave ?   As for the manger in which He lay—well, our silence does it more honour than any poor words of

---

[1] *Ep.* xxii. 38.   [2] *Ep.* cxxv. 20.   [3] *Ep.* xxii. 38.

ours. . . . Will the day ever dawn when we can enter
His cave to weep at His tomb with the sister (of Lazarus)
and mourn with His Mother ; when we can kiss the
wood of His Cross and, with the ascending Lord on
Olivet, be uplifted in mind and spirit?"[1]

Filled with memories such as these, Jerome could,
while far away from Rome and leading a life hard for the
body but inexpressibly sweet to the soul, cry out :
" Would that Rome had what tiny Bethlehem possesses !"[2]

But we rejoice—and Rome with us—that the Saint's
desire has been fulfilled, though far otherwise than he
hoped for. For whereas David's royal city once gloried
in the possession of the relics of " the Greatest Doctor "
reposing in the cave where he dwelt so long, Rome now
possesses them, for they lie in St. Mary Major's beside
the Lord's Crib. His voice is now still, though at one
time the whole Catholic world listened to it when it
echoed from the desert ; yet Jerome still speaks in his
writings, which " shine like lamps throughout the world."[3]
Jerome still calls to us. His voice rings out, telling us
of the super-excellence of Holy Scripture, of its integral
character and historical trustworthiness, telling us, too, of
the pleasant fruits resulting from reading and meditating
upon it. His voice summons all the Church's children
to return to a truly Christian standard of life, to shake
themselves free from a pagan type of morality which
seems to have sprung to life again in these days. His
voice calls upon us, and especially on Italian piety and
zeal, to restore to the See of Peter divinely established

[1] *Ep.* xlvi. 11.   [2] *Ep.* liv. 13.
[3] Cassian, *De Incarnatione* vii. 26.

here that honour and liberty which its Apostolic dignity
and duty demand.   The voice of Jerome summons those
Christian nations which have unhappily fallen away from
Mother Church to turn once more to her in whom lies all
hope of eternal salvation.   Would, too, that the Eastern
Churches, so long in opposition to the See of Peter,
would listen to Jerome's voice.   When he lived in the
East and sat at the feet of Gregory and Didymus, he said
only what the Christians of the East thought in his time
when he declared that " If anyone is outside the Ark of
Noe he will perish in the overwhelming flood."[1]   To-day
this flood seems on the verge of sweeping away all human
institutions—unless God steps in to prevent it.   And
surely this calamity must come if men persist in sweeping
on one side God the Creator and Conserver of all things !
Surely whatever cuts itself off from Christ must perish !
Yet He Who at His disciples' prayer calmed the raging
sea can restore peace to the tottering fabric of society.
May Jerome, who so loved God's Church and so strenu-
ously defended it against its enemies, win for us the
removal of every element of discord, in accordance with
Christ's prayer, so that there may be " one fold and one
shepherd."

[1] *Ep.* xv. 2.

G

Epilogue

DELAY not, Venerable Brethren, to impart to your people and clergy what on the fifteenth centenary of the death of " the Greatest Doctor " we have here set before you. Urge upon all not merely to embrace under Jerome's guidance Catholic doctrine touching the inspiration of Scripture, but to hold fast to the principles laid down in the Encyclical, " Providentissimus Deus," and in this present Encyclical. Our one desire for all the Church's children is that, being saturated with the Bible, they may arrive at the all-surpassing knowledge of Jesus Christ. In testimony of which desire and of our fatherly feeling for you we impart to you and all your flocks the Apostolic blessing.

Given at St. Peter's, Rome, September 15, 1920, the seventh year of our Pontificate.

BENEDICTUS PP. XV.

Printed in England

www.ingramcontent.com/pod-product-compliance
Lightning Source LLC
Chambersburg PA
CBHW022035080426
42733CB00007B/843